This Book
CONFESSIONS
of A
Teenager

Is A Loving Inspirational Gift To

_____

FROM

_____

Because nothing gives a child a greater advantage for their tomorrow, than feeling better about whom she or he is today!

Pamela Salaam Jaha
Aunty and Editor

FIRST EDITION - FIRST PRINTING

AUGUST 21, 2008

ISBN# 156411-510-0………..YBBG# 0529
ISBN# 978-156411-510-2

PUBLISHING CONSULTANT
H. Khalif Khalifah KHABOOKS.COM

Printed
In
Canada

Confessions
of A
Teenager

An Anthology of one of those things most
People …
Pastors, Parents, Preachers & Teachers
find hardest to face …
The Truth*

Featuring Harriet's Heart

Published and Edited by
SAI, Salaam Arts & Inspiration LLC
5dollarBilliondollarbooks

··

··

SAI, Salaam Arts & Inspiration LLC
PO Box 755 College Station NYC NY 10030

www.salaamartsandinspiration.com
Salaammeanspeace@aol.com

Some days
I go to bed worrying,
about all the terrible things, that happen in
this world.

In my dreams,
I remind myself to tell somebody
to do something about it.

Then I **WAKE UP**

and Remember

That Somebody,

Can Be Me!

Salaam

FOREWORD

Though small in size, this book is worth your weight in gold... maybe even both our weights. Why, because this book is born of Courage... Boundless Courage... a Courage you cannot buy at your 24 hour convenience store, in Hollywood shops or on the World Wide Web. This book is born of the Courage of Girls... leading lady warrior girls, Great, Intelligent, Real Life Soldiers *(as Taquisha would say)* who are brave enough to, after submitting their entry into this book, possibly face the judgements of society OR adults who feel children should be seen and not heard OR the backlash of family members who want to keep family matters in the closet OR clergy who may say having these feelings are a sin. These girls, the 15, 16 and 17 year old authors of these Confessions', yes, they have Boundless Courage. Because, greater than facing all the possible naysayers, these girls have the fire it takes to look themselves straight into the eye, facing their own past with a whole true heart and still having the wherewithal to grow up to become the great people they want to be and not who others life journeys, tried to define them to be. That is why I call them My Hearts ...

My Brave Harriet *(Tubman)* Hearts.

On my first day of nursery school, my teacher smiled at my mom when she dropped me off. That same day at lunchtime, she grabbed me by the back of my dress and slapped my face, because I did not like the taste of beets. She then told me how ugly my beautiful dress was, then smiled and waved again, when mom picked me up. At the age of 8, I knew my 3rd grade teacher had "low self esteem", even though I had yet learned that term. Feeling as ugly as she obviously did, she still had the audacity to discriminate. I loved my afro puffs, anyway. In 4th grade, my fur coat wearing teacher got frustrated each time she had to announce the winner of the spelling bee and it was me. When the students cheered for me one time too many, she took my book bag away and made me carry my school supplies and 9 large hardcover textbooks home, "like the chocolate monkey tomboy that I was". I stopped participating in class.

In junior high, the guidance counselor said, my being a quiet child, must mean that my dad was having sex with me. I was just trying to behave and learn, like my soft spoken mother and father. In high school, I was bored with an unchallenging half day schedule. It was then I began having sex. Even though it was not my plan or idea, nor did I know what the hell I was doing (he didn't either), I was now at least "occupied", especially since my friends said "everyone else is doing it". Finally, in college, my professor refused to read or grade my paper, on the premise that I was so charming, that the great things in my life obviously came far too easily for me. She decided she would help me fit in better, by making my life, "appropriately tough".

I was a wife and mother of 2 girls at age 23, yet it was when I made 27 that I discovered what it meant to be a real woman. So, I became a whole parent! My sister died unexpectedly at age 36. Although she loved the military and served diligently, they denied her request to be buried in the marine cemetery. At 35, I resigned from the organization I worked for since I was 14. They did not value my service either, so I turned my part-time work with hundreds into a fulltime enterprise serving thousands! At a business conference with other "successful" female entrepreneurs, I was asked, "how do you make any money while you still wear natural hair? And it was not until I reached 40, that I wholeheartedly embraced one of the most significant realities ever. The Truth, The Whole Truth and nothing but The Truth, Heals!

Most people have never had the opportunity to make confessions... to tell the truth... to purge themselves of experiences that hurt so bad, that they perhaps, unconsciously, translated those experiences into actions that hurt and oppressed loved ones, colleagues, clients and neighbors. How different might my life be, if those who influenced my growth and development, had the chance to purge truth, to confess their pains and fears, before influencing me?

This Book, this Manifesto "Confessions" is Dedicated to You... the teens of yesterday, today and tomorrow, because, being a teenager in any era, will always have it's "growing pains". Such is the nature of metamorphosis ... maturity. Though dramatic in content, this is a read intended to help the hurt start healing. We pray that some no longer feel alone on their journeys and still others are inspired to speak up, to say no to self destructive situations and behaviors and to say yes to the healing power of truth, communication and love. Parents, Pastors, Preachers and

Teachers, how far shall it go before we remember the value of holding babies in our arms and saying "Yes, I will always protect you, mind, body, heart and soul." before they go to touch the hot stove? Young people are growing up today, in difficult conditions that they, by the way, did not create. The very least we can do is to welcome their "unleash" and hear, with appreciation, their human voices. Like Martin and Malcolm said…

Let Freedom Ring … By Any Means Necessary!

So, to My Brave Hearts, Junise, Taquisha, Michelle, Denae, Priscilla, Teqwona, Tai, Dominique, Shanna, Jay and Khalia …I will always stand up for you and every other young person in the global scope of my soul! And no matter what, I Will Always Love You. **Aunty Salaam***

....

CONFESSION

It is defined in the Merriam-Webster dictionary as:

1. a disclosure of one's sins in the sacrament of reconciliation.

2. A written or oral acknowledgment of guilt by a party accused of an offense.

In lieu of this world renowned, somewhat limiting definition AND In consideration of family members who are still in the process of learning to appreciate the Heart's courage to fulfill their individual greatness, you will find no names used in this work.

***Nevertheless,
such is only the case, until the Master says***

... Now!

Heart 1
I CONFESS…
I am not as together, as I portray myself to be.

I feel like I am confessing a sin. This is something I have never shared with anyone in my life before. I don't know if I have even accepted the confession myself. I feel like I have been hiding it all my life. I just don't want people to see me differently, than how I am trying to portray myself. Yes… I am ashamed, but through Aunty Salaam, we have learned, "Our words may help heal others".

I am the one with the 88 grade point average, the inspirational one, the one who can give a killer speech or slamming words of advice. I am the one who plays every sport and has countless awards. But the truth is, I'll have nothing to show for my greatness, if I am an "addict of the fix". I don't know how to control my fixes or how to stop them, but I do have ideas of how and why got they started.
Mainly, it's about my never feeling complete enough, like half there, half missing. When I used to feel hurt, I would cut my arms until they bled. I would scrape and scrape, as though it wasn't my flesh that I was scraping. I would not stop cutting away with needles, pins, or staples until I saw a deep enough wound that would make my eyes cry dry and then … fall asleep… sometimes with the needle still in my hand. Why? It's a way to release what I was going through, to have my mind concentrated on another pain… a pain that I controlled, seeing how my life was already spinning wildly… without my permission.

Unfortunately, it does not stop there. When I am hurt, I also drink and smoke until I am so immune to the high that I forget why I was even sad to begin with. But even when I am drunk enough that I am unable to walk straight, there is still a voice in my head that reminds me of my pain. So, I drink more and more until I can't remember anything, until I am not living, just alive.

I don't hate many things, because hate carries a strong power that actually comes from weakness. Normally, I refuse to show weakness, but I can't help that my pain reveals that exact weakness in which I try so desperately to shield. I run around my life with smiles, while inside I walk with frowns. I confess. I am unable to deal with my pain, because I don't know how to. I confess that I tell others not to cut, smoke or drink because it will scar their skins, inside and out and not erase the underlining problem. I confess that I know my behavior makes me an emotional wreck. I know the side effects. I know it harms the body. Yet, I do it to make me feel better. If I did not, I don't know if I would be alive to share my confession today.

My "fix" helped me when I wanted to jump out my room window, after an argument with my mother about our distant relationship. It helped me when I was raged with anger about a boy who I thought I would end up marrying, but took my heart, used it, then dropped it like a hot plate. It helped me when I realized my eyes were never going to be blue or even green.

When I cut or drink or smoke, I feel a release of tension through my body. I am unsure if the chemicals in the cigarettes or liquor cause that, but then again, maybe not, because I get the same exact feeling when I cut and that carries no chemicals than that of my own. So I guess the release is only in my mind. It's kind of that feeling that you get when you know that if you eat another double layered chocolate cake its going to clog your organs with its fatty sugary grams. Still, you eat it anyway because it tastes so good. Yes, it's beginning to happen with food too. I count my calories, and check the labels, like I don't want to be fat. I don't want to be like a stick figure either. I just want to stay the way I am, but I realize I'm losing less and less weight. I don't want to be anorexic or anything. I just want to be thin like I am. F---, there I go again. That's how my other addictions started. Even in relationships I do this s---, knowing the stupid ass ain't right for me or only wants one thing and I get with him anyway.

For some reason I have hope that everything will be alright if I cut once more, drink another 40, smoke another cigarette, not eat another fry, kiss another boy or act dumb just one more time. I am addicted to the rush I get when I feel better by something else because I myself am not always able to "fix" it. I am not a smoker or an alcoholic or a cutter. It could be anything, its not the thing I am addicted to, it's the "f ix" I get during it. I could name numerous fixes. Trouble is they only work for the moment. The scar on my lower wrist is proof that the pain did not go away. God, it still hurts! I still don't know how to deal with the hurt so I confess that I have committed a sin, a crime, not according to the bible or the government, but according to the spirit world. It hurts. I cry. But, I know your tears too. Those tears when you feel like giving up and quitting the task of this universe. When you feel like you are standing alone and no one f---ing understands your pain. I know about being a Miss-Understood child! I am crying right now, because it gets so hard that I wonder how I am to handle all the baggage, laid in front of me making my soul so heavy.

You can! You can! I say to myself. I know you are stronger than you think, than you feel, than you know! Don't you want a fix, something healthy that lasts? I know I do. I pray to God that I find my cure, because these sick fixes are wearing me out.

I am proud of myself. I didn't cut today and when a friend offered me a cigarette, I said "No". Yes!!! It's getting better.

Message: Destruction of your body is not good structure for dealing with your pain. Hope, Faith and Love of God, assures that there will always be better days.

Heart 2
I CONFESS …
To the dislike of my mom, the year I turned 13!

When I was a child, my mother was a beautiful lady. She took care of herself and had a new hairstyle every other week. Not only that, we had a good relationship. We would go out to eat and we had a connection that no one could take away. Every daughter knows a bond with their mother is one of the most valuable things she could have. When I looked into my mother's eyes, I could see happiness and contentment. She partied a lot, but that was okay because I knew we would always have time to be together again. I remember the times when she would get ready to party and I would just sit there and stare at her. Once she would leave I would walk around with her high heels and I felt so grown. She would leave me with my grandmother and return any time. My mother, grandmother, step grandfather and I lived in the same apartment. I was happy for my mother because she was having so much fun. My grandmother took care of me, so either way, I still had the attention a child needs from their family.

It was around fifth grade when I witnessed my mother's first nervous breakdown. One day hell came knocking at my family's door. He was tall, big and had a look of mischief in his eyes. He claimed he knew my mother for a while, but I had never seen anything like him before. When I looked at him I saw pure evil and deceit. However, that was not my mother's case. She looked at him like he was some jewel. Please! Time went by. My mother began to spend more time with him in Queens and less time with me at home. I began to notice she would buy him plenty of unnecessary things to satisfy his wants. Things like an X-box. What grown man needs an X-box?

One day my family was planning our annual trip to Richmond Virginia. On the day of that trip, my mother decides to take me with her to Queens to see this guy. I have been to his place many times before, so I was familiar with my surroundings. I would usually nap on the couch downstairs, but for some reason he told my mom to have me sleep in the room with the two of them. I thought of this as awkward because I don't even sleep in the same bed with my grandparents. It just seems so wrong. I tried to decline, but my mother wanted me up there. In that room, my mother laid in between me and him. As I began to drift off to sleep, I felt a hand on my breast. I elbowed the person in their stomach. I looked at my mother and she was sleep. It was him, that nasty pig.

The morning came and when he left I told my mother what he had done to me last night. She said she would speak with him when he returned. When he arrived I went downstairs while she spoke to him. My mother called me back up and told me what I said was false. Did she know how much that hurt? The worst part is, from the look in her eyes, I know she actually believed him. At that moment, I contacted my grandmother to make sure she did not leave me to go down south yet. Luckily she didn't.

A year from that incident, we were back on our trip to Richmond when we received a call. It was a call from my mother saying he put a gun in her mouth. As a reaction, she had a nervous breakdown. We returned back home and she was put in the hospital immediately. I learned then that this was not her very first nervous breakdown. Her first one occurred when my great-grandfather died. He and mom were very close. When he died, my mother did not know how to cope and she took it very hard. This was before I was born though. Anyway when I saw my mother in the hospital, I was horrified… horrified, because I had never seen my mother like that before. My grandmother would constantly go and see her to make sure everything was fine. A couple weeks later when she felt better, I was happy to see her, but to my surprise, she was still in search for him, that beast of a person. I could not believe it. Still, after all he had done to her, she went back to him. I may have been a teenager, but I was not naive.

A year later the craziness started... the year my mother informed my family she was moving down south with him. Was she deranged? It was bad enough he was abusing her right here in New York, but to move away where he could abuse her and we'd have no way to get to her. She moved. I was devastated.

As she began to settle in her new home, she would call us everyday. Her voice seemed so distant though. I could tell she was bored and she needed her family. She told me all she did there was sleep and eat. She would always want to talk to me, but my interest for her faded. I did not want to talk to her and I hardly ever called. While she was with him, she was a whole different person. She could not see what I could. He would constantly call her skinny and said that she revealed to much skin. She began to take weight gaining pills and over eating just so she can please this man. When she returned back to New York to visit, she looked horrible in my eyes. She was now fat and she was dressed in baggy men clothes.

I was through, so anytime she would say something to me I would have an attitude. On many occasions we got into it. I mean we really fought. I fought back because I was mad. I was mad because she neglected me. Mad she put me at the end of her list, while she put him at the top. Mad because she forgot her daughter, her only blood daughter. He took away a bond between my mother and I and she let him.

As of today, that man is in jail. He is in jail for gun possession and my mother is back in New York with me and my grandparents, where she should have been all along. I am growing up now.

I confess that I was afraid that I may grow up to be just like her… schizophrenic. The dislike I had for my mom has simmered down… mostly because I want to be healthy and not have the same mental sickness. Yes. We are working on strengthening our bond. But he still has this pull on her … even behind bars.

Message: Have faith in knowing how great you really are. You are not your parents' illnesses, challenges or bad decisions. You don't even have to grow up to be just like them. Focus on the good things in your life, the love they were/are capable of giving and live each day to the best of your own capability. Accept and ASPIRE!

Heart 3
I CONFESS …
My suburban life is not as perfect as it is perceived to be.

Many people are under the impression that suburban girls are spoiled brats and live a perfect stress-free life. They think we are rude, disrespectful, and throw a fit whenever we don't get our way. Well, I am here to clear up all of the assumptions. Truth is, we go through the same problems as any other teenage girl… from friends to boys all the way down to family problems. In suburban towns, contrary to what some may believe, we even have deaths and tragedies. In that, I have come to realize, suburbanites are actually naive. We just don't believe certain things will happen in our towns. Truth is, they really do.

Two summers ago a neighborhood boy that I knew was shot and killed at a house party in my town. The murdered boys were in a gang from a neighboring town about fifteen minutes away. The whole town was in total shock because they never imagined a tragic event like this happening in our neighborhood... the suburbs. I personally was shocked and a little terrified because it happened about five blocks away from my house.

I go to parties all the time and was just imagining that I could have possibly been at this party. It is unbelievable that you could let your child go to a party and later that night get a phone call that they were shot. Since that happened, my parents have become more overprotective, when it comes to what parties I attend. Before I am able to go to one, they always want to know who is going and if people outside of my community are going. That is a hard situation because you never know who is going to show up to a party. Sometimes people that are not invited attend parties. How do you decide to go or not? How do I even admit that I am afraid?

This second event was more tragic to me because it happened to someone I am close to and love. My brother was slashed in his head with a blade at a party. He was at a party in the next town over from us and a fight broke out between some people. He tried to move away from it and when he bent down to pick up his camera and phone that he dropped someone slashed him in his head. He was rushed to the hospital and had to get stitches. When I heard what happened I was really sad and then at the same time nervous about ever going to parties again.

Yes, suburbanites are looked at by ourselves and others, as privileged. Yet, how do I explain how I feel to other kids who think we have it made? How do I admit that I am now afraid of going to parties, without looking like a, "well"? I don't know how to face or make kids who don't live in the so called "luxury" of the suburbs, understand, that I do not live a PERFECT life.

Message: Be honest. Don't be afraid to express your feelings, it will allow you to get things off of your chest. Besides, to most people, the grass is always greener, on the other side of the fence.

HEART 4
I CONFESS …
To a whole year of deep depression,
while the rest of the world thought I was happy.

When I was 3 years old my parents parted. I remember the screams and the blood trail from my mom's room into the living room. Drops of red sorrow flowed from my father's nose. I was so petrified that I still remember this as if it were yesterday. One moment I saw him walking down the hallway and the next minute I saw men in white suits with a bed, laying my father down, and putting him in the elevator with my older sister leaving with him. I remember running out of the apartment door and crying to leave with them, but my mother screamed at me and wouldn't let me. I thought my dad was out of my life forever. The next thing I know I'm thinking my mother is out of my life forever, for my dad returned for me and we never looked back. As the details are told to me now…me and my father left and slept in our car. What I remember is my dad bringing me to my uncle's house. I lived with them in the projects. All I knew were the projects, until we moved into a little apartment in a 3 family home.

We had to move again because the government would not allow my dad and I to share the same room. The social workers would ask me questions to see which parent should take me and I remember the nervousness of saying something wrong. They might think my mother was better for me and THAT I dreaded because at the time, I hated my mother. Everyone taught me to. My dad wanted full custody and got it so easily, for my mother didn't even bother showing up to the court hearing. We then moved to a beautiful two family house, and I had my own back yard and everything. At the time of my parents break up, my Dad owned his own business and would have to travel from downtown Manhattan every day, before and after school to drop me off and pick me up. I would always spend after school in my dad's office. Looking back now, I don't know how my father did everything, but all of this affected the future and how and who came into my life. Ironically, that contributed to my depression in the year of 07'.

My father eventually grew weary from everything, so he found me a baby sitter. She was very pretty and slender with the most gorgeous dark hair. I loved the way she looked, but stepping foot into that world became exhaustion for me. I experienced mental torture, for the first time. This babysitter lady slowly became my "step mother". Years past and I and my father moved in with my step family. There were constant words of torture all day, until my father came home from work. Once home, we'd all have mad fun, but it went right back to torture as soon as he left me there to go to work again.

All I ever wanted, all my life, was to have a larger family than just me and my dad. When we moved into my step mother's house, with her two children close to my age, I thought having a family would be the greatest joy I had ever had. Instead, my stepmother was nasty toward us, implementing all these rules and reminding us that the house that we had just moved into was hers. Me and my dad took this crap and kept it moving. We experienced fun times there but those fun times came to an end once we realized that the two separate families that tried to combine had a different way of living. Regarding us children, my dad would not allow friends in the house every single day, but my step mother would. He would not allow me to go out whenever I wanted and hang with guys. My step mother would. My step-mother never made me feel like she accepted me as her daughter, but saw me as a part of my father's package. She soon just became "That lady". We began to argue and that lady showed me what the devil looks like. She would say horrible things and her two kids would follow. My dad in wanting revenge would do the horrible things right back. I always thought revenge was childish because then you stoop down a level...but I started to feel it. My dad was trying hard to keep the so called family together. Still, we walked around a whole month ignoring each other not speaking a word unless it was absolutely necessary, and then guess what? We got thrown out! We got thrown out, just like my mother did to me and my father.

I felt so betrayed, for we trusted these two woman and they abandoned us for their own selfish reasons. I never felt so cheated in my life! I felt very hurt and grew depressed. I thought me and my dad were going to have to live in a car again, for we had no place to go. I even gave up on my dream of having a mother and family. Then I became upset, when I recalled that my dad had so much money from selling his business and winning a lawsuit. We could've owned a house right now, yet he spent it all because he let "that lady" tell him what to do with his money. My father had to borrow money from all over the place, even from loan sharks. My dad just grew into so much debt that I felt selfish even asking for lunch money. When I needed clothes or something I would not ask for it. I'd rather not have what I needed than to ask. My heart dropped at seeing my dad suffer again, the same symptoms he had with my mom…waterfalls of tears. I felt responsible for my fathers' happiness. I was his best friend. And as if this experience wasn't enough, I was in charge of my mother's heart at the same time.

My mother would call me late at night to tell me how her new husband beats her, cheats on her and steals her money. She even told me she couldn't even sleep from fear of being raped. If you were to hear her desperate cries for help you would understand why I was so depressed! So much pressure was put on me that I felt as though I was preparing for both of my parents burial. She hated the way she looked and the way she lived her life. She began to tell me how she was jealous of me… jealous of the life I had versus the life she never had. She believed she did not deserve a better husband or good enough to get a job, since she couldn't even work with children because of a previous conviction. She told me that my older sister was in a shelter. That year is when I found out the whole truth about her conviction and the lies were all revealed and I was hurt, again.

I felt that the two people that loved me so unconditionally did not realize the pain they caused me, I know they didn't. I know I appeared so strong to every one, so happy to everyone, and maybe that's why they kept telling me things … because I was both my mothers and fathers only friend and actually, I was probably the only person to listen.

I started to pick up my mother's habits of hating myself, and not liking the way I looked. I started to hate every part of my body and wish that I looked different. When I finally began to heal from the madness, my mother called me from a party … drunk. She had my youngest sister with her and left my other little sister, who's not the rightful daughter of her boyfriend, at home alone with him. On that day I wrote…

Dear Mom,
Why must you always remind me that you are suicidal and that you don't want to live for anyone, not even me? Then, say that you're not right up there and that you belong in a psychiatric ward… declaring all you want for you burial is flowers. But, then you call me your savior! Thanks, but how good of a savior am I if you still want to die?

You know, although I was playing out my depression as happiness every where I could, one day, my dad did notice and ask "What's the matter? You don't seem so happy any more?"… and I said "What are you talking about?"…and that was it. Funny how easy it was to turn suspicion into "okay its nothing… maybe she just had a bad day". One time me and my dad went to the doctors office, and they gave ME a questionnaire, but my dad wanted to do it for me, like, at the time he liked to do everything for me. It came to the question "do you have friends that smoke?"…he checked no…"have you ever experienced depression?"…he checked no. That made me so mad that he was so clueless. So clueless that in my school when they gave everyone in my grade a stress and depression test, I said I didn't want to take it because it makes no sense for me to take because I am happy! He believed and agreed with me. He didn't even realize I just took myself out of a situation of being discovered.

My mother would consistently tell me after saying she is depressed "but you wouldn't understand, you're too young to know about depression". I always wondered if she saw my soaked pillows at night… if she saw my daily routine of crying myself to sleep, would she continue to believe that, then?

From then on, I did a lot of things to heal myself, myself. I started to realize that I cannot help any one unless they want to help themselves. It is their life. I can love them but I have to care about my well being too. I began smiling, because it felt happier than faking a frown. I would look at myself in the mirror and keep telling myself I was beautiful, until I actually believed it. I started telling my best friends how I truly felt and sought advice. I traveled, and started to do more and more community service. Those two extra-curricular activities brought more than shine to my world, they brought exposure… exposure to new people, places and things! I was introduced to new ways of seeing, hearing, feeling and thinking. Most of all I learned that in some experiences, you may have to learn to ACCEPT instead of always trying to fix it or understand.

As of right now my mom is addicted to her sleeping pills and things for her life haven't changed that much. Sometimes she owns up to her life and wants a change and is actually making an effort to improve. This makes me so proud. My heart still shatters when I have to leave my sisters teary faces caused from separation. I take more responsibility on getting on the train and seeing my mother and little sisters in Harlem and coming back home to my Bronx building. My dad still sees "that lady". Her daughter and I get along better now. My dad still struggles with money but he never gives up on us, ever.

I have the greatest parents in the world, for although I saw and went through more than I could ever put on paper…the experience that they brought upon my life has made me wiser and stronger. At the end of it all, I know they never, never meant to hurt me.

*Message: My mentor once told me "if you want to see the change, you've got to be the change!" Thanks Aunty Salaam!

Heart 5
I CONFESS…
I Don't Love My Body, because it is not the best.

Body image is a struggle among teenagers across the country. It has gotten so bad that it is even true for guys as well as girls. Me… I am just another one out of a million.

Although I am intelligent and outgoing, deep down I struggle with my outward appearance. Girls complain that they are fat and they wish they looked like a model … slim and trim, with long beautiful dark hair, like me! Little do they know that I wish I was thick. I WISH I WAS THICK, WITH CURVES!

I look at other girls with big butts and big breasts and I wonder why don't I have all of that. Some girls have those beautiful feminine curves and waste it with their head down the toilet, throwing up their last meal, trying to get a flatter stomach. My stomach is flat and I am still not happy with my body. These girls have it all, body and brains. So why are they still miserable?

I know I have to be grateful for what I have. I thank God for life and being a healthy young lady. Still, I want to feel pretty too. I want to feel attractive. I want those looks, the looks guys give girls when they walk down the block. Why don't I get them if I am so healthy? Or why is it that I'm always remembered as this girls little friend or that girl from your school. If I had a curvier body would guys remember my name?

Would I feel better?

Message: Your body is what you are blessed with. We are chosen to look differently. Would it be fun if we all looked the same? Don't let the opinions or the pressures of others keep you down. Love those who love you for who you are. Every body type can be beautiful, if you take great care of the inside and the outside. Count your blessings, eat well, exercise and rock with it, roll with it!

Heart 6
I CONFESS…
My Body is asking for something and I think it's… Sex!

I am now 17 years old and I am feeling really different after the incident with my parents 2 years ago… when I first fell in love. For some strange reason, I feel as if my body is asking for something. There are times when I feel that my body is begging for something but I am not sure what. Hmmm?

I am now dating one of the most beautiful people I have ever met in my life. I knew he was going to play a very important role in my life when I realized that I went to his house on my trip to Florida in 2007.

I was traveling with family and friends when we went to his house and met his whole family … except for him. I was told later that he was sleeping and got up when we left. Amazing, right? I was there for about 3 hours and he was sleeping that whole time. When he got up, his family began telling him about who was there, about me and what I looked like. He was interested. He knew one of my cousins and some other people that I knew. He started investigating and finally found someone who had my email. He messaged me and told me who he was.

We started getting really close over the internet. It was okay, especially because our families knew each other very well. We finally met and it was one of the greatest moments in my life. The connection was so different from any I have experienced before. Right there and then, I knew I was going to love him.

Our parents approved of our relationship, so we started dating officially. Because he was in Florida and I was in the Bronx New York, there was a distance between us that caused us to miss each other. When we finally got to see each other in person, I kissed him. When we kissed, it felt like it had the potential to go further. Naturally, we stopped it before letting it go that far.

Now back to my body asking for something. It may just be my body asking for my boyfriend's presence, but honestly i don't think that's all to it. I don't really know how a person knows they are ready for sex but I think my body is 10 steps ahead of my age. I have the desires to do things that I have never done before. I don't want to do it because I know the situation I went through with my family almost 2 years ago. Still… I also want to do it to see if it will satisfy this curiosity and my body too. Ugh, I don't know what to do and I'm sure there are many other teens that go through this, but a handful of them do it without thinking and get pregnant. Well … regardless of what this may be, I am going to wait a while longer before I have sex. Yep … That's probably the best thing to do.

Wow. Now that I'm thinking, I haven't seen my boyfriend in 7 months. Hmmm. I know a kiss will turn into something else. One great thing about him is he is afraid to take it that far with me because I am involved in so many things. I am at the top of my class and deeply involved in my afterschool, weekend and future career programs. He doesn't want to be the one who helps me destroy my life or slow it down. He will help me fight temptation until we are ready to have sex!

Back to what my body wants. Do you think its sex?

Message: When trying to make a decision, know that the answers will come from both your heart and your head. Pay attention, learn the difference and follow what's closest to your soul.

Heart 7
I CONFESS …
I am Not that Innocent!

It all started on a warm summer Friday in September. I planned on going over to my 19 year old "boyfriend's" house to braid his hair. I called him up, he met me by the 4 train and we went to his house. We talked watched movies, played video games, listened to music and were just having fun, until things got a little more advanced. I don't think he was planning on me staying as long as I did, and I know I wasn't expecting to, but in the midst of time I wasn't thinking about it.

Ironically, we were sitting on his bed watching the 40-Year-Old Virgin. I was just 14. Us being a "couple" we'd kiss here and there, but these weren't ordinary kisses. These kisses were more passionate… more meaningful, I guess you could say. We were lying down and items began to disappear. Now in my head, I'm thinking its 8pm. I should be on my way home. But, for some reason, I couldn't leave. This has happened before, where a guy has asked or tried to have sex with me but in those cases I was always quick to say no. So what was different in this situation? 'Until this day, I still don't know.

After it all was done, I kept thinking to myself, "What will my parents say? What will they do when they find out that I am no longer a virgin? What am I going to say when they ask me "why didn't you answer your phone and where were you until 11:00 at night?" The questions just kept coming and soon the visualization of being beaten half to death came into play. So… I stayed. Yep! That's right, I said it. I stayed.

Things would have been better if I would have at least called someone to calm their worries, but I was afraid!!! He asked me continuously "Are you sure you don't want to call home?" That night it was hard for me to sleep. I could only think of my mom and how she must be feeling. As we laid, we talked and he rubbed my back until I fell asleep.

The next morning he took me home. Well... not really. He rode the bus with me and then we went our separate ways. I called my mom from a pay-phone and told her everything that happened. Her reply was "Don't worry baby. I'm just glad that you are okay". She called my dad and he came with my grandfather to come pick me up. Surprisingly, he didn't kill me on the spot. He hugged me and talked to me for a very long time and then we went home. They didn't kill me... even though they called the police, filed a missing persons report and all. They didn't even yell (that day), but I was on punishment for as long as I could remember! My father made me call my "boyfriend". He had a real long talk with him. Yes, he threatened him. He even paid him a visit at his job.

My first lover is no longer my boyfriend and for the next few weeks, I received "The Talk" from every adult I knew. Phew ... I learned a lot!

*Message: Your body is your temple... a precious gift from God. Sex does not mean love. No one can treat you or love you better than you can treat or love yourself. Most parents and family will be there, through your growing pains and life lessons. Trust them because they care, even if they don't agree with your choices. Don't sneak or disappear. Believe it or not, parents hurt too and at the end of the day, only want the best for you.

Heart 8
I CONFESS...
My family is the Cause and the Cure to my pain.

Have you ever wanted to tell your parents something but thought it was easier to sneak around? That was definitely me!!! I believed that it was so much easier to ease my way around the truth, rather than facing it like the "G" that I am, LOL.

One day I went to go meet a boy that I was really interested in. It just so happened to be 11:30 at night. I thought I was real sneaky, because it was my mom's birthday and my parents had gone out to dinner. When they arrived home around 1 am, I was no where to be found. I was just 15 years old and I was out having a night on the town, experiencing new things, with the new boy in my life.

Go figure...

Today, I am torn into pieces at the fact that my father still refuses to reconnect with my sister after she choose a boy over him... a boy who tried to harm him (our father) over her. Now, she no longer lives with us. He says it hurts him, but the more he sees my sister the less it hurts, which means soon he won't even acknowledge her as his first born child. This is tearing my heart to shreds! I love them both. I want my family back! F--- the boy! I am in a tug of war with my only sister and my father. I know they both love me and want the best for me. I know I shouldn't be sneaky and deceitful by sneaking behind my parents back but I AM SCARED. I never imagined us, my family, in this situation. The worst part is that no one understands exactly what I'm going through. I miss my sister. I miss my family being together!

Sometimes I just sit in my room and cry because things get so lonely.....and they have the nerve to wonder why I'm always on the phone and why my texting bill was through the roof. I'm bored, DUH! Meanwhile, I'm stuck wearing a smile on the outside and a wounded heart on the inside. DAMN! Why cant things just fall into place like they did before I became a TEENAGER?

I have something that I need to say. I know that if I don't tell my parents, I risk losing my parents along with losing my sister. If I do tell them, they will believe that I am turning into a liar, just like my sister and our relationship will still end up messed up. Only God knows when I will get up the courage to tell them what I am holding inside. Maybe this confession will be a start. And then maybe ...

Message: Family is a treasure. Hold treasures near. Then do the right thing, so they don't disappear!

Heart 9
I CONFESS ...
I feel stupid. It was my fault. I did not tell.

Both of them did it... though at different times. I felt the same way each time it happened... used and abused. Yes. I was molested!! Yes me... I know, but it was my fault. You see, I didn't say anything. Well, up until now that is.

One night I fell asleep on my oldest brother's bed. I had to be at least ten years old. He was about 13. I was in there because that's where the TV was. Anyway. I was asleep. I don't know for how long, but I know it was late.

I felt someone on top of me. I took a peek... it was my older brother. He was humping on me, feeling on me even moaning in my ear. By that time, I was fully awake, just laying there, acting like I was sleep. I didn't know what to do. After a couple of minutes of him pleasing himself, he ejaculated all over my shorts. I laid there in disgust crying inside. I was f---ing furious, but I didn't have the heart to say anything.

Why did he do that? Why did he make me feel like I was just a dummy doll that someone used as a sex toy? I didn't know, but I didn't dare tell my mother. Now... some may call me stupid for this one.

I was also touched by my youngest brother. Yup. You read it right... my youngest brother. I had to be about eleven of twelve so he was maybe seven or eight. We used to share the same room. Why? I don't know, but we did.

One afternoon I was taking a nap. Yet again I was sleeping on my brothers' bed. My bed was broken and mommy hadn't replaced it yet. I was sleeping when I felt him in back of me. I didn't think anything of it. Who would have thought he'd have such a perverted mind at age seven? He started moving on me and rubbing my butt. Yet again, I laid there acting sleep. He did this for a couple of minutes. I guess he wanted more action, so he pulled my pants down as best as he could, pulled his little dirty penis out and started his motion again. After a while, I felt him trying to stick his little thing in my butt. It never worked. I felt so low when he would kiss my neck. But I still didn't do anything. I didn't even move. I just laid there being touched in places I was scared to look. Why didn't I do anything? Why didn't I stop what was happening to me? I guess I was too afraid of what would happen next. I was afraid to tell because I didn't know how it would make me look.

For a long time after that, I dressed like a boy, never letting either of my brothers get too close. I even did boyish things to prevent boys from liking me. I was a tomboy who never combed her hair let alone wore clothes that matched. I hated myself for allowing those things to happen to me. I cried all the time as I was growing up. How could my own brothers touch me and fill me with disgust the way they did? I was so ashamed.

Because of this, I stopped dancing. I used to love to dance. Ballet, hip hop everything. Now, I don't like to dance or move my body in front of other people at all, because I don't want attention on my body parts. It took me a long time to allow myself to have a real boyfriend. I used to be so paranoid. I thought I had AIDS or a STD or something... not educated enough to realize that nothing really went inside of me.

Today I'm older, wiser and I'm not a passive little girl anymore. I'm now letting the whole world know what happened to me in my past. I'm not afraid to confess the truth. Although I still feel uneasy when I dance, I won't let my past take complete control of my future. Boy that felt good... no, not that silly. Telling the truth! Only God knew what was happening to me. Of course, my brothers did too. After all these years of keeping my secret, it feels GREAT to finally let it out! It's funny how today I RELEASED IT and I don't hold a grudge, but I'll be damned if they'd try something like that again! It's 2008 and I kept quiet about this way too long. Now... it's time to let the brothers and myself, out of the bag!

Message: Don't hold on to experiences from friends or loved ones that are not good or true. Be motivated, courageous and free yourself, knowing that your best friend is you!

Heart 10
I CONFESS...
I want to Hate her, but I Can't, because I Love her.

My mother is a b---- and I hate her! I can't wait until I turn 18 so I can leave!! I don't want to have anything to do with her! Every little thing I do, she wants to make it seem like I'm wrong, even when it's really her. I'm tired of everyone saying I have to listen to her because she is my mother. F--- her!

Today she upset me so, so much. If she's going through something, it's like I have to go through it too. She tried to take my property that she didn't even pay for. How can you justify taking something away from me that YOU didn't pay for? Exactly!!! You can't!! Then she tried to kick me out because of it!! She actually took my keys and my phone. It's funny to me, because the things I do compared to my brother are not half as bad. Still, I am always in a bunch of trouble. I can't wait until he's older, so she can realize that he is worse than me… and then…

I am going to LAUGH at her stupidity! She hates me. Well, I guess as bad as I want to hate her, but I can't. I can't because I love her so much and just I HATE to admit that because… because I know she just can't wait to get rid of me. It's only when I do something wrong that she pays attention to me. When it comes to other peoples kids, she knows I am good. So why is my mom so ungrateful? I am hurt. I am angry. And to top it all off, the thing that I hate the most about myself is… I want her to love me. I want her to love me back, because I love her so very much. I always want her to be proud of me and be an important part of everything that I do. I want her to say "That's my baby" and smile and hug me and tell me how much she loves me, everyday, all the way, no matter what!

MOMMY CAN YOU HEAR ME? You are My World. You are My Inspiration and My heart! YES Mommy, you are my heart. So…why mommy? Why do you hate me? Why do you have to hate me so much? Why do you have to hate me so much, that my unconditional love for you… is now…   my biggest downfall?

Message: Stop trying to fit in, when you were meant to stand out!

Heart 11
I CONFESS...
I've tried to be "Normal" for so long, but "Normal" never made me happy.

Three years ago I entered high school. It was in high school that I became curious about trying new things. I did things I thought I'd never do. Things like … kiss a girl, yes a girl!

Everyone thought I was boy crazy, but I was putting on a disguise. Truth was, the boys were the ones crazy for me! For so long I hid from my loved ones what I truly liked and what I truly preferred. One day I asked my mother what she would do if I was attracted to the same sex, I remember her response. It will be forever clear in my head. She said "I'd disown you! My daughter will not and can not like girls".

From that day forward I decided to force myself to be with guys, whether I enjoyed it or not. I wasn't really attracted to many. Yes, I thought some were cute, but when it came down to it there was never really any chemistry.

I confess. It didn't make sense to me why I liked females. On some nights I cried myself to bed, I longed to be "normal" like everyone else. I was tired of holding this in. I was tired of making everyone believe I was boy crazy. I fell asleep crying because I felt I didn't fit in. I fell asleep crying because I didn't want to be looked down upon. I fell asleep crying because I just wanted to be "NORMAL" but I did not know HOW?

For a long time I thought that if I had sex with a guy I would grow to like him. I tried it. Once it didn't work, I'd go out with another guy and he'd want me to have sex with him, so I would. After a while I began to notice I was being taken advantage of. I didn't like it, but I didn't know how to stop it. I tried convincing myself that being with a guy no matter what was the best thing. Up until last week, I think I even told myself I was going to be with a guy even if it killed me… then, it almost did.

I was in a relationship with a guy for about 1year and 8 months. I thought I had found the guy to change my mind about liking females, because at first things were really great. Then again, all things start off great don't they? As we went into dating for 1year and 2 months we began to argue a lot. He became very controlling and jealous. I felt shut down like I had to ask permission to do things I enjoyed … I had to be careful with each and everything I did and said.

One day, I got the courage to leave him. I was ready to be true to my own feelings and heart. He cried and said he couldn't live without me. He showed up at my house and just wouldn't leave. He threatened to crash his car and kill himself. Okay, now I was scared. The pressures, the decisions, everything got really out of hand. Things became so overwhelming at this point, that I wanted to die. I wanted to kill myself and I tried.

I confess. There were a few nights where I laid in my bed, with a cut arm, hoping to bleed to death. But, I was too afraid to die. Believe it or not, lying there, hoping that things would get better. Hoping that I would find the strength to be true to myself, seemed to keep me alive! Yes, my fear of dying saved me. I thank God that it did.

Today, I am in the process of recovering. Although the experience has traumatized me, I can still stand and say, I am somewhat proud to be who I am. I am still in the process of being true to myself. No, I am not as strong as I used to be, because I am afraid that showing who I really am, will hurt my family. Still, I am working on it.

How do you hide something like this from the people you love? If they don't accept it, do they really love you in return? Did they ever love me or just who they thought I should be? Can I go the rest of my life hiding my true feelings? Do I even want to?

*Message: Don't try to live a life that is not yours. You can only truly live, if your soul is truly happy. **Baby… the Heart don't lie!***

………………………………………………….

We pray that this book of Our Truths,
have moved you to
"Help your Hurt start Healing".
Wishing You Joy, Faith, Peace, Protection, Truth & Courage… Aunty Salaam and the Courageous Girls of **Harriet's Heart…** Great, Intelligent, Real, Life, Soldiers (as Taquisha would say)!

P.S. We Love You!

*Feel **INSPIRED** to use this space to write your own*
Confession(s)

Today's Date: _____

_____
_____
_____
_____
_____
_____
_____
_____
_____
_____
_____
_____
_____
_____
_____
_____
_____
_____
_____
_____
_____
_____
_____
_____
_____
_____

Harlem New York Entrepreneur
Adopts 19 Teenaged Girls

On November 5, 2005, Pamela Salaam publicly announced her surrogate adoption of 19 teenaged girls, whom she lovingly calls, Harriet's Heart. Harriet's Heart is a groundbreaking 4 year undertaking, honoring the legacy of Harriet Tubman. 19 especially selected young ladies, each representing Tubman's 19 courageous journeys on the Underground Railroad, are guided from girlhood to womanhood via *leadership and life skills readiness, social etiquette and artistic expression,* assuring successful completion of high school, then onto the freedom of academic exploration. A goal is to raise over $1 million dollars in cash and resources to support their college educations! *"I know it is the responsibility of all of us to lead our children, families and communities to social leadership, economic strength, political promise and academic excellence! In honor of Harriet Tubman, forward thinking journeys must continue. I know that ordinary people can make a change. Such is when and how we become Extra-Ordinary",* says the proud surrogate mother of 19, Salaam! Harriet's Heart is a primary component of GirlSpirit WomenSong Inc., a non profit 501C3 charity founded by Ms. Salaam. GSWS Inc. is the philanthropic arm of SAI, Salaam Arts & Inspiration.

All we need are 1000 ANGELS!!! **Please make Tax Deductible Donations PAYABLE to GSWS Inc. Mail to GirlSpirit WomenSong Inc. PO Box 755 College Station NY NY 10030 OR Donate by PayPal @ www.salaamartsandinspiration.com Salaammeanspeace@aol.com www.youtube.com/saihearts**

Salaam's Entrepreneurial Endeavor is as Founder/CEO of SAI
Salaam Arts & Inspiration LLC

SAI designs and implements curriculum, programs & personal and professional development seminars for students and adults.Native New Yorker and product of the NYC public school system, Salaam strategized her "life purpose" career, becoming a Contracted Vendor with the NYC Department of Education, to birth then champion initiatives that energize both the classroom and the workplace by combining the arts with life learning experiences. SAI's direct services are both coeducational and gender specific, addressing "real life" needs. Creative genius Salaam too facilitates enterprising workforce development opportunities for city/state agencies, individuals, private groups, corporations, educators, parents and artists of all genres that:

♥ *Build Confidence,*
♥ *Improve Public Speaking*
♥ *Promote Team Building,*
♥ *Encourage Critical Thinking,*
♥ *Inspire Forward Thinking,*
♥ *Support Workplace/Classroom Productivity,*
♥ *Motivate social responsibility& change!*

SAI inspires taking a proactive role in your own life, emphasizing progressive life choices and the elaboration of basic human competencies for healthy growth and development!